# Healing the Frontlines:
## The Art of Military Medical Leadership

Anup Halappanavar

In "Healing the Frontlines: The Art of Military Medical Leadership," military doctors will find a comprehensive guide to enhancing their leadership abilities in the dynamic and demanding field of military medicine. This book aims to provide valuable insights, practical strategies and inspiration to empower military doctors to make a profound impact on the lives of their patients, lead their healthcare teams effectively, and leave a lasting contribution to the profession.

Anup Halappanavar
Belgaum, Karnataka
anupsdmedic@gmail.com

*"Healing the Frontlines: The Art of Military Medical Leadership" provides military doctors with valuable insights, practical strategies and inspiration to enhance their leadership abilities in the challenging and rewarding field of military medicine.*

*Since many doctors are already entrained into administrative role no matter which organization they are part of or even private practitioners, for that matter, this book aims to identify key areas for learning and mindful practice.*

*I sincerely hope that this book shall help the reader identify key areas for sharpening of skills to be able to lead their teams from the front in all situations. In this regard, readers will realize that the principles encoded in this book apply not just to military environment, but also to any organization which the leader is an extension of.*

*By mastering the art of leadership, military doctors can profoundly impact the lives of their patients, empower their healthcare teams and make a lasting contribution to the profession of healthcare.*

Chapter 1: Introduction to Military Medical Leadership

- The significance of leadership in military medicine
- Unique challenges and opportunities for military doctors
- The power of effective leadership in saving lives and fostering a resilient healthcare team


Chapter 2: The Foundation of Military Medical Leadership

- Understanding the military healthcare system
- Embracing the core values of military service
- Developing a personal leadership philosophy
- Balancing compassion and professionalism


Chapter 3: Leading Yourself

- Self-awareness and self-reflection
- Setting personal and professional goals
- Maintaining physical and mental resilience
- Effective time management and work-life balance


Chapter 4: Building and Leading High-Performing Teams

- The importance of teamwork in military medicine
- Creating a culture of trust, respect, and open communication
- Recruiting and developing exceptional healthcare professionals
- Nurturing diversity and inclusion in your team

Chapter 5: Leading Through Crisis and Adversity

- Preparing for and managing medical emergencies and disasters
- Making critical decisions under pressure
- Communicating effectively in high-stress situations
- Supporting and inspiring your team during challenging times

Chapter 6: Ethical Leadership in Military Medicine

- Upholding ethical standards in patient care

- Balancing the demands of military objectives and patient welfare
- Addressing moral dilemmas and ethical challenges
- Building a culture of integrity and professionalism


Chapter 7: Leading Change and Innovation

- Embracing a mindset of continuous improvement
- Initiating and managing change in healthcare delivery
- Fostering innovation and creative problem-solving
- Overcoming resistance to change

Chapter 8: Mentoring and Developing Future Leaders

- The role of mentorship in military medical leadership
- Identifying and nurturing leadership potential in others
- Providing constructive feedback and coaching
- Creating a legacy of leadership excellence


Chapter 9: Leading in a Global Context

- Collaboration with international partners and medical
  organizations
- Understanding cultural differences and adapting leadership
  approaches
- Participating in humanitarian missions and peacekeeping
  operations
- Contributing to global health initiatives


Chapter 10: Personal Growth and Lifelong Leadership

- Embracing lifelong learning and professional development
- Networking and building relationships within the military
  medical community
- Transitioning from military service to civilian healthcare
  leadership
- Leaving a lasting impact on military medicine

# 1

# Introduction to Military Medical Leadership

In the world of military medicine, leadership plays a vital role in ensuring the delivery of exceptional healthcare to service members, their families, and even civilian populations during times of crisis. This chapter delves into the significance of leadership in military medicine, highlighting the unique challenges and opportunities faced by military doctors. It also emphasizes the power of effective leadership in saving lives and fostering a resilient healthcare team.

1.1 The Significance of Leadership in Military Medicine: Military medical leadership goes beyond traditional healthcare leadership roles. It encompasses the ability to make critical decisions in high-stress environments, manage limited resources, and adapt quickly to rapidly changing situations. Leaders in military medicine are entrusted with the lives of their patients and the well-being of their teams, making their roles inherently significant.

1.2 Unique Challenges and Opportunities for Military Doctors: Military doctors face a distinct set of challenges and opportunities that set them apart from their civilian counterparts. They operate in dynamic and unpredictable environments, often providing care in austere conditions or during combat operations. Additionally, military doctors must navigate the complex military healthcare system, work within the framework of military command structures, and address the specific health needs of a diverse and transient population.

1.3 The Power of Effective Leadership in Saving Lives and Fostering a Resilient Healthcare Team: Effective leadership is a force multiplier in military medicine. Strong leaders inspire trust and confidence, enabling their teams to perform at their best, even in the face of adversity. Through skilled leadership, military doctors can optimize the delivery of healthcare, streamline processes, enhance patient outcomes, and ultimately save lives on and off the battlefield. Furthermore, effective leaders cultivate a culture of resilience, supporting their teams' well-being and fostering a cohesive and adaptable healthcare workforce.

Conclusion: Leadership is a fundamental component of military medicine. It brings together the unique challenges and opportunities faced by military doctors, emphasizing their vital role in the provision of healthcare within the military context. By recognizing the significance of leadership, understanding the specific challenges they may encounter, and harnessing the power of effective leadership practices, military doctors can become influential leaders who positively impact the lives of their patients and the success of their healthcare teams.

# 2

# The Foundation of Military Medical Leadership

Introduction: Building a strong foundation is crucial for military medical leaders to navigate the complex and demanding landscape of their profession. This chapter explores the fundamental elements that form the bedrock of military medical leadership. It begins with understanding the military healthcare system, followed by embracing the core values of military service. Additionally, it delves into developing a personal leadership philosophy and striking the delicate balance between compassion and professionalism.

2.1 Understanding the Military Healthcare System: Military medical leaders must have a comprehensive understanding of the military healthcare system. This includes knowledge of the organizational structure, chain of command, and key stakeholders involved in delivering healthcare services to military personnel. Understanding the unique aspects of military healthcare, such as deployment medicine, trauma care, and the integration of military and civilian healthcare resources, allows leaders to effectively navigate and optimize the system for the benefit of their patients and teams.

2.2 Embracing the Core Values of Military Service: The military is guided by core values such as integrity, loyalty, duty, respect, selfless service, honor, and personal courage. Military medical leaders must internalize and embody these values, serving as role models for their teams. Embracing these core values fosters a culture of professionalism, ethics, and self-discipline, which are essential for effective leadership within the military healthcare setting.

2.3 Developing a Personal Leadership Philosophy: A personal leadership philosophy serves as a guiding compass for military medical leaders. It encompasses their beliefs, values, and principles, providing a framework for decision-making and actions. By reflecting on their experiences, strengths, and areas for growth, leaders can develop a philosophy that aligns with their personal values and professional aspirations. A well-defined leadership philosophy provides clarity, consistency, and authenticity in leadership practices, inspiring trust and confidence in those they lead.

2.4 Balancing Compassion and Professionalism: Military medical leaders must strike a delicate balance between compassion and professionalism. While demonstrating empathy, compassion, and sensitivity to the needs of their patients, they must also uphold the highest standards of professionalism, maintaining objectivity, integrity, and ethical conduct. This balance ensures that leaders can provide the best possible care while also preserving the discipline and efficiency required in military healthcare settings.

Conclusion: The foundation of military medical leadership lies in understanding the military healthcare system, embracing the core values of military service, developing a personal leadership philosophy, and striking a balance between compassion and professionalism. Armed with this solid foundation, military medical leaders can navigate the complexities of their profession, inspire their teams, and deliver exceptional healthcare while upholding the principles and values that define military service.

# 3

# Leading Yourself

Introduction: Effective leadership begins with self-leadership. Military medical leaders must prioritize their own personal and professional development to lead others effectively. This chapter explores the essential components of leading oneself. It emphasizes the importance of self-awareness and self-reflection, setting meaningful goals, maintaining physical and mental resilience, and practicing effective time management and work-life balance.

3.1 Self-awareness and Self-reflection: Self-awareness is the foundation of personal growth and effective leadership. Military medical leaders must engage in self-reflection to gain insight into their strengths, weaknesses, values, and areas for improvement. By understanding themselves better, leaders can leverage their strengths and mitigate their weaknesses, making informed decisions and leading authentically.

3.2 Setting Personal and Professional Goals: Goal-setting is vital for personal and professional growth. Military medical leaders should establish clear and achievable goals that align with their vision and values. By setting specific, measurable, attainable, relevant, and time-bound (SMART) goals, leaders can track their progress, stay motivated, and continuously strive for improvement.

3.3 Maintaining Physical and Mental Resilience: Military medical leaders operate in demanding and high-stress environments. It is essential to prioritize physical and mental well-being to maintain resilience. Leaders should engage in regular exercise, maintain a healthy lifestyle, and seek support when needed. Additionally, cultivating resilience through mindfulness, stress management techniques, and self-care practices equips leaders to navigate challenges and inspire resilience in their teams.

3.4 Effective Time Management and Work-Life Balance: Effective time management is crucial for military medical leaders to optimize their productivity and maintain a healthy work-life balance. Leaders should prioritize tasks, delegate when necessary, and establish boundaries to prevent burnout. Balancing professional responsibilities with personal interests and family commitments allows leaders to sustain their well-being and lead by example, demonstrating the importance of work-life harmony.

Conclusion: Leading oneself is an essential aspect of military medical leadership. By cultivating self-awareness and engaging in self-reflection, leaders can harness their strengths and address areas for growth. Setting personal and professional goals provides direction and motivation for continuous improvement. Prioritizing physical and mental resilience ensures leaders can navigate challenges and inspire their teams effectively. Lastly, effective time management and work-life balance enable leaders to maintain their well-being and sustain their leadership effectiveness. By leading themselves, military medical leaders lay the groundwork for leading others and making a significant impact in their healthcare organizations.

# 4

# Building and Leading High Performing Teams

Introduction: Military medical leaders are responsible for cultivating high-performing teams that can deliver exceptional healthcare in demanding and dynamic environments. This chapter explores the essential elements of building and leading such teams. It emphasizes the importance of teamwork in military medicine, creating a culture of trust, respect, and open communication, recruiting and developing exceptional healthcare professionals, and nurturing diversity and inclusion within the team.

4.1 The Importance of Teamwork in Military Medicine: Teamwork is the cornerstone of success in military medicine. Collaborative and cohesive teams are essential for delivering timely and effective healthcare. Military medical leaders must emphasize the interdependence of team members and foster a collective sense of purpose, emphasizing that every individual contributes to the overall mission. Effective teamwork enhances communication, coordination, and synergy among healthcare professionals, resulting in improved patient outcomes.

4.2 Creating a Culture of Trust, Respect, and Open Communication: A strong team is built upon a foundation of trust, respect, and open communication. Military medical leaders must establish a culture where team members feel safe to express their ideas, concerns, and feedback. By actively listening, providing constructive feedback, and valuing diverse perspectives, leaders foster an environment where open dialogue and collaboration thrive. Trust and respect are nurtured through consistent actions that demonstrate fairness, integrity, and empathy.

4.3 Recruiting and Developing Exceptional Healthcare Professionals: Military medical leaders play a crucial role in recruiting and developing exceptional healthcare professionals. By selecting individuals who possess the necessary skills, values, and commitment to service, leaders lay the foundation for a high-performing team. Additionally, leaders should provide ongoing professional development opportunities, mentorship, and feedback to help team members reach their full potential. Investing in the growth and development of healthcare professionals enhances their skills, knowledge, and motivation, ultimately benefiting the team and the patients they serve.

4.4 Nurturing Diversity and Inclusion in Your Team: Diversity and inclusion are essential aspects of a high-performing team. Military medical leaders should actively foster an inclusive environment that values and respects differences in background, experiences, and perspectives. Embracing diversity enhances creativity, innovation, and adaptability within the team. Leaders must promote equal opportunities, ensure fairness, and challenge biases or discrimination. By nurturing diversity and inclusion, leaders create a team that reflects the diverse patient population they serve and enhances cultural competence in healthcare delivery.

Conclusion: Building and leading high-performing teams is a critical responsibility for military medical leaders. By emphasizing the importance of teamwork, creating a culture of trust, respect, and open communication, recruiting and developing exceptional healthcare professionals, and nurturing diversity and inclusion, leaders foster a cohesive and effective team. A high-performing team not only delivers exceptional healthcare but also enhances the morale, engagement, and well-being of its members. Through their leadership, military medical leaders can inspire and empower their teams to achieve remarkable results in the pursuit of providing outstanding care to those they serve.

# 5

# Leading Through Crisis and Adversity

Introduction: Military medical leaders are often called upon to lead their teams through crisis and adversity. This chapter explores the essential skills and strategies required to effectively navigate challenging situations. It covers preparing for and managing medical emergencies and disasters, making critical decisions under pressure, communicating effectively in high-stress situations, and supporting and inspiring the team during challenging times.

5.1 Preparing for and Managing Medical Emergencies and Disasters: Military medical leaders must be well-prepared to handle medical emergencies and disasters. This includes conducting thorough planning, training, and simulations to ensure readiness. Leaders should establish clear protocols, allocate resources effectively, and coordinate with relevant stakeholders to provide timely and efficient healthcare in crisis situations. By maintaining a state of readiness and practicing proactive measures, leaders can effectively respond to emergencies and save lives.

5.2 Making Critical Decisions Under Pressure: In crisis situations, military medical leaders often face the need to make critical decisions under extreme pressure. Effective decision-making requires a calm and rational approach. Leaders should gather all available information, assess risks, consider various options, and consult with relevant experts when necessary. Decisions must be made swiftly, considering the best interests of the patients, the team, and the mission. Leaders should also be prepared to adapt their decisions as circumstances evolve.

5.3 Communicating Effectively in High-Stress Situations: Clear and effective communication is paramount in high-stress situations. Military medical leaders must convey information accurately and in a timely manner, ensuring that everyone understands their roles and responsibilities. Effective communication involves active listening, providing clear instructions, and utilizing appropriate channels and technologies. Leaders should also remain approachable and empathetic, encouraging open communication within the team and addressing any concerns or anxieties that may arise.

5.4 Supporting and Inspiring Your Team During Challenging Times: During times of crisis and adversity, military medical leaders play a vital role in supporting and inspiring their teams. Leaders should demonstrate empathy, compassion, and appreciation for the efforts of their team members. By acknowledging the challenges they face and providing emotional support, leaders can boost morale and maintain team cohesion. Additionally, leaders should provide opportunities for debriefing, reflection, and self-care to ensure the well-being and resilience of the team.

Conclusion: Leading through crisis and adversity is a significant responsibility for military medical leaders. By preparing for and managing medical emergencies and disasters, making critical decisions under pressure, communicating effectively in high-stress situations, and supporting and inspiring the team, leaders can successfully navigate challenging circumstances. Effective leadership during crisis situations not only saves lives but also instills confidence, resilience, and unity within the team. By exemplifying strong leadership qualities, military medical leaders can overcome adversity and provide exceptional care even in the most challenging circumstances.

# 6

# Ethical Leadership in Military Medicine

Introduction: Ethical leadership is of utmost importance in the field of military medicine. This chapter explores the critical role of ethical leadership in ensuring the highest standards of patient care and professionalism. It covers upholding ethical standards in patient care, balancing the demands of military objectives and patient welfare, addressing moral dilemmas and ethical challenges, and building a culture of integrity and professionalism within the healthcare team.

6.1 Upholding Ethical Standards in Patient Care: Military medical leaders have a responsibility to uphold ethical standards in patient care. This involves maintaining patient confidentiality, respecting autonomy, and ensuring informed consent. Leaders must prioritize patient well-being above all else and ensure that the medical decisions made are in the best interest of the patient. By adhering to ethical guidelines and promoting a culture of ethical conduct, leaders set the example for their team and maintain the trust of their patients.

6.2 Balancing the Demands of Military Objectives and Patient Welfare: Military medical leaders often face the challenge of balancing the demands of military objectives with the welfare of their patients. It is crucial to navigate this delicate balance with integrity and compassion. Leaders must ensure that the medical needs of service members are addressed while upholding ethical principles. This requires open communication with military command, advocating for the needs of patients, and making well-informed decisions that prioritize patient care within the constraints of the military context.

6.3 Addressing Moral Dilemmas and Ethical Challenges: Military medical leaders may encounter moral dilemmas and ethical challenges that require thoughtful consideration and decision-making. These dilemmas could involve issues such as allocation of limited resources, end-of-life decisions, or participation in controversial medical procedures. Leaders must approach these challenges with ethical frameworks, seeking input from ethics committees or consultation services when necessary. By engaging in robust ethical discussions and considering the perspectives of stakeholders, leaders can navigate these complex situations while upholding the highest ethical standards.

6.4 Building a Culture of Integrity and Professionalism: Military medical leaders play a pivotal role in building a culture of integrity and professionalism within the healthcare team. Leaders should foster an environment where ethical conduct is valued and expected. This involves promoting open dialogue, encouraging ethical decision-making, and providing opportunities for ethical education and training. By setting high standards of professionalism, leaders inspire their team members to uphold ethical values, reinforcing a culture of integrity throughout the organization.

Conclusion: Ethical leadership is essential in military medicine, as it upholds the highest standards of patient care and professionalism. By prioritizing ethical standards in patient care, balancing the demands of military objectives and patient welfare, addressing moral dilemmas and ethical challenges, and building a culture of integrity and professionalism, military medical leaders create an environment that promotes ethical conduct and ensures the well-being of patients. Through their ethical leadership, military medical leaders inspire trust, foster professionalism, and uphold the values that are fundamental to the practice of medicine within the military context.

# 7

# Leading Change and Innovation

Introduction: In the ever-evolving field of military medicine, leaders must be adept at leading change and fostering innovation. This chapter explores the crucial role of military medical leaders in driving change and promoting innovation within healthcare delivery. It covers embracing a mindset of continuous improvement, initiating and managing change, fostering innovation and creative problem-solving, and overcoming resistance to change.

7.1 Embracing a Mindset of Continuous Improvement: Military medical leaders must embrace a mindset of continuous improvement to adapt to changing circumstances and deliver the best possible care. This involves cultivating a culture of learning, encouraging feedback and reflection, and promoting the adoption of evidence-based practices. By fostering a culture of continuous improvement, leaders inspire their team members to seek opportunities for growth, refine processes, and enhance the quality of care provided.

7.2 Initiating and Managing Change in Healthcare Delivery: Initiating and managing change in healthcare delivery requires strong leadership skills. Military medical leaders should clearly communicate the need for change, engage stakeholders, and establish a shared vision for the desired outcomes. Leaders must provide support and resources to facilitate the implementation of change initiatives and address any concerns or resistance that may arise. By effectively managing change, leaders ensure the successful integration of new practices and processes that improve patient care and operational efficiency.

7.3 Fostering Innovation and Creative Problem-Solving: Innovation is essential for advancing military medicine. Leaders must foster an environment that encourages innovation and creative problem-solving. This involves promoting a culture that values new ideas, collaboration, and experimentation. Leaders should create platforms for sharing innovative practices, provide resources for research and development, and recognize and reward innovative efforts. By fostering innovation, leaders inspire their teams to find novel solutions to challenges and improve the effectiveness and efficiency of healthcare delivery.

7.4 Overcoming Resistance to Change: Resistance to change is a common challenge in any organization. Military medical leaders must address resistance by listening to concerns, providing clear communication about the rationale and benefits of the proposed changes, and involving stakeholders in the decision-making process. Leaders should anticipate and address potential barriers, provide support and training to facilitate the transition, and address any misconceptions or fears that may arise. By effectively managing resistance to change, leaders can create an environment where change is embraced and sustained.

Conclusion: Leading change and fostering innovation are critical for military medical leaders to drive continuous improvement in healthcare delivery. By embracing a mindset of continuous improvement, initiating and managing change, fostering innovation and creative problem-solving, and overcoming resistance to change, leaders can shape the future of military medicine. Through their leadership, they inspire their teams to embrace change, contribute innovative ideas, and deliver exceptional care in the face of evolving challenges. By cultivating a culture of change and innovation, military medical leaders ensure that the healthcare provided to military personnel is of the highest quality, efficiency, and effectiveness.

# 8

# Mentoring and Developing Future Leaders

Introduction: Mentoring and developing future leaders is a vital responsibility of military medical leaders. This chapter explores the critical role of mentorship in military medical leadership, including identifying and nurturing leadership potential in others, providing constructive feedback and coaching, and creating a legacy of leadership excellence.

8.1 The Role of Mentorship in Military Medical Leadership: Mentorship plays a significant role in fostering the growth and development of future leaders in military medicine. Mentors provide guidance, support, and wisdom based on their own experiences. They serve as role models, helping mentees navigate their career paths, develop leadership skills, and overcome challenges. Mentorship cultivates a culture of learning and continuous improvement, ensuring a pipeline of capable and confident leaders in military medicine.

8.2 Identifying and Nurturing Leadership Potential in Others: Military medical leaders have the responsibility to identify and nurture leadership potential in their team members. This involves observing individuals' strengths, qualities, and commitment to service. Leaders should provide opportunities for growth, delegate responsibilities, and encourage individuals to take on leadership roles. By investing in their development, leaders can groom future leaders who will carry on the mission of delivering exceptional healthcare.

8.3 Providing Constructive Feedback and Coaching: Effective mentors provide constructive feedback and coaching to help individuals develop their leadership skills. Leaders should offer feedback in a timely and specific manner, highlighting strengths and areas for improvement. They should also provide guidance and resources to help individuals enhance their leadership competencies. Through coaching, mentors help mentees develop self-awareness, refine their decision-making abilities, and strengthen their communication and teamwork skills.

8.4 Creating a Legacy of Leadership Excellence: Military medical leaders can leave a lasting impact by creating a legacy of leadership excellence. They should strive to inspire and empower their mentees to become leaders themselves. This involves sharing knowledge, experiences, and lessons learned, while encouraging mentees to surpass their own achievements. Leaders should promote a culture of collaboration and support, where leaders at all levels are committed to developing others. By fostering a legacy of leadership excellence, military medical leaders ensure a sustainable leadership pipeline and a resilient healthcare system.

Conclusion: Mentoring and developing future leaders is a crucial responsibility for military medical leaders. Through mentorship, leaders can identify and nurture leadership potential in others, providing guidance and support to help individuals grow and develop their leadership skills. By providing constructive feedback and coaching, leaders empower mentees to reach their full potential. Ultimately, by creating a legacy of leadership excellence, military medical leaders inspire a new generation of leaders who will continue to deliver exceptional healthcare and uphold the values of military service.

# 9

# Leading in a Global Context

Introduction: Military medical leaders operate in a global context that requires them to collaborate with international partners, understand cultural differences, participate in humanitarian missions and peacekeeping operations, and contribute to global health initiatives. This chapter explores the unique challenges and opportunities of leading in a global context and provides guidance on how military medical leaders can effectively navigate these situations.

9.1 Collaboration with International Partners and Medical Organizations: In a global context, military medical leaders must collaborate with international partners and medical organizations to enhance healthcare capabilities and share knowledge. This involves building strong relationships, fostering mutual trust and respect, and establishing effective communication channels. Leaders should actively seek opportunities for collaboration, such as joint training exercises, information sharing, and research partnerships. By embracing collaboration, military medical leaders can leverage the collective expertise and resources of international partners to improve healthcare outcomes.

9.2 Understanding Cultural Differences and Adapting Leadership Approaches: Leading in a global context requires an understanding of cultural differences and the ability to adapt leadership approaches accordingly. Military medical leaders should educate themselves about the cultures and customs of the regions they operate in, demonstrating cultural sensitivity and awareness. They should be open-minded and flexible, willing to adjust their leadership style to accommodate diverse perspectives and values. By adapting their leadership approaches, leaders can build stronger relationships, promote inclusivity, and facilitate effective teamwork.

9.3 Participating in Humanitarian Missions and Peacekeeping Operations: Military medical leaders often participate in humanitarian missions and peacekeeping operations, providing healthcare in areas affected by conflicts or natural disasters. These missions require leaders to demonstrate compassion, resilience, and the ability to adapt to challenging environments. Leaders should ensure the safety and well-being of their teams, prioritize the needs of affected populations, and collaborate with local authorities and organizations. By leading with empathy and effectiveness in these missions, leaders can make a significant impact on the lives of those they serve.

9.4 Contributing to Global Health Initiatives: Military medical leaders have the opportunity to contribute to global health initiatives that aim to improve healthcare on a global scale. This involves engaging in research, participating in international conferences and forums, and advocating for policies and practices that address global health challenges. Leaders should stay informed about emerging issues, collaborate with experts and organizations, and leverage their influence to drive positive change. By actively contributing to global health initiatives, military medical leaders can play a pivotal role in advancing healthcare worldwide.

Conclusion: Leading in a global context requires military medical leaders to collaborate with international partners, understand cultural differences, participate in humanitarian missions and peacekeeping operations, and contribute to global health initiatives. By embracing collaboration, demonstrating cultural sensitivity, participating in humanitarian missions, and engaging in global health initiatives, leaders can make a significant impact on healthcare outcomes and promote global health security. Through their leadership, military medical leaders can foster international cooperation, enhance healthcare capabilities, and contribute to the well-being of people around the world.

# 10

# Personal Growth and Lifelong Leadership

Introduction: Personal growth and lifelong leadership are essential aspects of military medical leadership. This chapter explores the importance of embracing lifelong learning and professional development, networking and building relationships within the military medical community, transitioning from military service to civilian healthcare leadership, and leaving a lasting impact on military medicine.

10.1 Embracing Lifelong Learning and Professional Development: To thrive as military medical leaders, it is crucial to embrace lifelong learning and continuous professional development. Leaders should seek opportunities for further education, attend conferences and workshops, and stay updated on advancements in medical research and technology. By continually expanding their knowledge and skills, leaders can provide cutting-edge care, make informed decisions, and inspire their teams to pursue excellence.

10.2 Networking and Building Relationships within the Military Medical Community: Networking and building relationships within the military medical community is vital for personal growth and effective leadership. Leaders should actively engage with colleagues, superiors, and subordinates, both within their own branch of service and across different branches. Networking opportunities can include professional conferences, interagency collaborations, and mentorship programs. By fostering relationships, leaders gain valuable insights, access to resources, and support from a diverse community of military medical professionals.

10.3 Transitioning from Military Service to Civilian Healthcare Leadership: At some point, military medical leaders may transition from military service to civilian healthcare leadership. This transition requires adaptation and leveraging the skills and experiences gained in the military. Leaders should seek opportunities for professional development and training that address the unique challenges of civilian healthcare leadership, such as navigating different organizational structures and financial models. By effectively transitioning, leaders can continue making significant contributions to the healthcare field beyond their military service.

10.4 Leaving a Lasting Impact on Military Medicine: As military medical leaders progress in their careers, they have the opportunity to leave a lasting impact on military medicine. This involves mentoring and developing future leaders, sharing knowledge and experiences, and advocating for positive changes within the military healthcare system. Leaders should strive to create a culture of excellence, innovation, and compassion, ensuring the continuity of outstanding care for military personnel. By leaving a lasting impact, leaders contribute to the ongoing advancement of military medicine and the well-being of those they serve.

Conclusion: Personal growth and lifelong leadership are critical components of military medical leadership. By embracing lifelong learning and professional development, networking and building relationships within the military medical community, transitioning from military service to civilian healthcare leadership, and leaving a lasting impact on military medicine, leaders can continually evolve and make significant contributions to the field. Through their commitment to personal growth and lifelong leadership, military medical leaders inspire their teams, advance healthcare practices, and positively impact the lives of military personnel and their families.